James K. Polk

James K. Polk

Sean McCollum

AMERICA'S
11TH
PRESIDENT

Children's Press®
A Division of Scholastic Inc.
New York / Toronto / London / Auckland / Sydney
Mexico City / New Delhi / Hong Kong
Danbury, Connecticut

Library of Congress Cataloging-in-Publication Data

McCollum, Sean.
    James K. Polk / by Sean McCollum.
        p. cm. — (Encyclopedia of presidents. Second series)
    Summary: A biography of the eleventh president of the United States, with
information on his childhood, family, political career, presidency, and legacy.
Includes bibliographical references (p.) and index.
    ISBN 0-516-22885-4
    1. Polk, James K. (James Knox), 1795–1849—Juvenile literature. 2.
Presidents—United States—Biography—Juvenile literature. [1. Polk, James K.
(James Knox), 1795–1849. 2. Presidents.] I. Title. II. Series.
E417.M1155 2003
973.6'1'092—dc22   2003015960

CHILDREN'S PRESS and associated logos are trademarks and or registered
trademarks of Scholastic Library Publishing. SCHOLASTIC and associated
logos are trademarks and or registered trademarks of Scholastic Inc.
1 2 3 4 5 6 7 8 9 10 R 13 12 11 10 09 08 07 06 05 04

Contents

Chapter 1

Under the Knife

Jimmy Polk was hurting. The 17-year-old farm boy had never been the picture of health. In fact, in the rough-and-tumble frontier life of Middle Tennessee, he was considered a sickly weakling. Now, in 1812, the pains in his abdomen had grown sharper. His parents were ready to try anything to help their eldest son. When news reached the Polk homestead about a Kentucky doctor using new techniques to treat similar problems, father and son saddled up.

The two rode their horses from their home in Tennessee 230 miles (370 kilometers) to Danville, Kentucky, to seek treatment from Dr. Ephraim McDowell. McDowell concluded that Jimmy had a stone in his gallbladder and suggested surgery to remove it. The trip had so exhausted Jimmy Polk, however, that he needed to recover before the operation could take place.

After Jimmy had rested for three weeks, McDowell strapped the boy to a wooden table. Jimmy was given several big swallows of brandy, a strong alcoholic drink, as a painkiller. Then assistants took a good hold of the boy's legs, and McDowell cut into the boy's abdomen. History does not record exactly what he

Medicine in 1812

Today a patient with gallstones would be given an anesthetic to put him to sleep, and the operation would be done in a brightly lighted, spotlessly clean operating room. A small army of medical technicians would be there to monitor his progress. Later, powerful drugs would help prevent infection.

Compared to this, medicine in Jimmy Polk's time seems like a form of torture. Since anesthetics had not been developed, the patient was given an alcoholic drink to numb the pain. Then he bit down on a piece of leather or a bullet as the doctor cut through his flesh. If patients survived the surgery, they still had to beat infection. Doctors did not know that microscopic creatures on their hands or instruments could cause life-threatening infections. They didn't clean their hands or surgical instruments before operating. Germ-killing drugs such as antibiotics had not been invented. Patients who lived through surgery often died later of infections.

Even with all the pain and danger, surgery was sometimes a lifesaver. Jimmy Polk owed his life and health to an adventurous doctor—and his own body's ability to resist infection and to heal.

☆ ★ ☆

did, but it is likely that the doctor removed the stone from Jimmy's bladder. Jimmy probably passed out from the blinding pain.

This agonizing ordeal proved a turning point in the future president's life.

Carolina Born

Jimmy Polk began life in western North Carolina, where the energetic and successful Polk family was an important part of the community. His grandfather, Ezekiel Polk, had done well in business, and had gained hundreds of acres of farmland in Mecklenburg County, near present-day Charlotte. His son Samuel married Jane Knox in 1794, and Ezekiel gave the young couple a 250-acre (100-hectare) farm as a wedding present. The next year, their first child, James, was born there in a log cabin.

Through hard work, and the work of the family's slaves, the farm prospered. Samuel became one of the young leaders of the community. There were no formal schools, so the Polk children learned to read and write at home. Sometimes a traveling teacher set up a "field school" for a few weeks. One resident remembered years later, "Little Jimmy Polk used to pass along this road often to school, barefooted, with his breeches rolled up to his knees. He was a mighty bashful little fellow."

A reproduction of the log cabin in Mecklenburg County, North Carolina, where Jimmy Polk was born and spent his childhood. The original cabin probably consisted of the center portion with a single door and window in the front.

In 1803, Jimmy's grandfather Ezekiel and four of his grown children moved across the Appalachian Mountains to the frontier lands in Tennessee with their families. Jimmy's parents stayed in North Carolina. Three years later, in 1806, Sam and Jane Polk, now with five children, loaded up some of their belongings, sold the rest, and set out on a month-and-a-half journey to join the other Polks on the frontier. Eleven-year-old Jimmy had to walk most of the 500 miles (800 km) to his new home.

Making and Taking Tennessee

In 1769, the first permanent white settlement was established in the lands that became Tennessee. Just 26 years later, in 1795, the region had 60,000 "free inhabitants" and applied for statehood, taking the name of an ancient Cherokee city. When the Polks arrived, Tennessee was still part of the wild, wild, west. Cherokee, Chickasaw, and Creek peoples hunted in the forests, often clashing with white settlers. Settlers themselves scratched out homesteads and farms far from the safety and convenience of towns.

As Native American nations gave up their lands to the United States, the trickle of settlers became a flood. In 1818, the year James Polk graduated from college, the Chickasaw sold the last of their Tennessee territory to the U.S. government. Polk would be elected to the Tennessee *legislature* (the elected body that passed its laws) and would represent his state in the U.S. Congress for years. As a legislator and as president, he was a strong supporter of the country's westward expansion.

☆ ☆ ☆

"The Most Promising Young Man" ———

Jimmy's family settled on land in the middle of the state, near the Duck River, about 40 miles (65 km) from Nashville. They brought down trees for the new log house, raised and built with the help of neighbors. They cleared the rich soil for planting their first crops. Jimmy helped chop down the wild cane that grew everywhere and popped like gunshots when thrown onto fires.

As frontier folk, living far from towns and stores, the Polks had to produce, find, kill, or make nearly everything they ate and used. That meant chores from sunup to sundown for Jimmy Polk and his brothers and sisters. Corn was the main food crop, supplying flour that could be baked into corn bread, hoecake, and sweet johnnycake. The Polks also raised tobacco, which they sold so that they could buy the things they couldn't raise, such as sugar, salt, and iron for tools.

Samuel Polk left much of the farming to the family and to slaves. He improved the family's finances by becoming a skilled *surveyor*. New settlers needed someone to measure where their property began and ended. Jim's dad provided that service, trudging through the backcountry with his equipment to map out the property. Often he was paid in acres of land instead of cash. Sam took his eldest son on some of these land surveys to try to teach him the trade. But often Jimmy was too sick to leave camp. Instead, he stayed behind to cook and look after the horses.

Small and pale, Jimmy Polk must have suffered periods of great pain from his illness. He was often unable to help with chores that required strength or endurance, and he couldn't play roughhouse games and sports with boys his own age. Because of his bouts of pain and poor health, Jim had to learn a different kind of toughness. He had been named after James Knox, his grandfather on his mother's side. The Knox family were devoted Presbyterians, and Jim's mother

Rutherford Creek, just behind the Polk homestead, where Polk may have played and fished.

had been raised in the Presbyterian faith. She taught Jim how to control his emotions and face his troubles with determination. She also burned into him ambition and a strong sense of duty that would serve him well throughout his life.

There might never have been a President Polk, though, if Dr. McDowell had not removed that gallstone. Jim's health improved dramatically after the surgery and he enjoyed a newfound burst of energy. He soon made up for years stolen by illness.

Shortly after Jim returned home from the surgery, his father arranged a job for him in a store in nearby Columbia, Tennessee. But being a merchant did not suit Jimmy. After a few days behind the counter, he talked his dad into sending him to school instead.

In July 1813, Jim Polk enrolled at a small school run at Zion Church in Columbia. He had never before been to formal classes, and at first it showed in his spelling and writing. But under the instruction of the Reverend Robert Henderson, Jim quickly proved himself a gifted and knowledge-hungry student, learning to read both Latin and Greek.

Jim's father saw that Jim was a talented student. The following year, Jim entered an academy (a kind of high school) in Murfreesboro. There he studied geography, philosophy, astronomy, and logic, and continued with Latin and Greek. He devoured his studies like a starving man at a banquet, and after a year he felt ready to go on to college. At the 1815 show to exhibit the academy students' talents, Jim gave a successful speech and was called "much the most promising young man in the school."

— In just two years, Jimmy Polk had made huge strides. He began as a sickly boy with a doubtful future, and now he was a hardworking scholar admired by his fellow students and ready to take on the world.

College

In fall 1815, a nervous Jim Polk arrived in Chapel Hill, North Carolina, to take the entrance examinations for the University of North Carolina. He had made great progress in his two years of schooling, but would those studies hold up during a difficult entrance exam of English grammar, Latin, and Greek? They did. Jim did so well on the exam he was allowed to skip ahead one year and entered the university as a sophomore.

An early paper cutout shows all the buildings at the University of North Carolina about the time James Polk enrolled there.

When Polk enrolled, the university was barely 20 years old and was still very small. It had a president, one professor, three tutors, and about 80 male students. Still, the demanding schedule and course work would have exhausted modern-day college students. At 6 A.M., the New College Bell rang, calling students to morning prayers. Lectures and lessons took up most of the morning and afternoon. Another bell at 8 P.M. sent students to their rooms for more study before sleep.

In his first year, Jim concentrated on the classics in Greek and Roman literature. His second year was devoted to mathematics, a subject for which he developed a passion. In his last year, he studied "natural and moral philosophy"—the study of science, religion, and ideas.

Some of his most important education came outside the classroom. He joined the school's Dialectic Society, a club that practiced public speaking, writing, and debate. Members were required to take part in a debate one week and submit an essay the next. Eight of Jim's essays won top honors. The society's competitions sometimes fired up Jim's temper—he and an opponent were fined for trading personal threats when one debate turned into a hot argument.

Jim was elected president of the Dialectic Society twice. As a senior, he delivered a speech describing how its activities prepared members for careers as ministers, lawyers, or politicians. In May 1818, he graduated first in his class. By that time, he knew exactly which of those careers he wanted to follow.

Chapter 2

Learning on the Job

In fall 1818, Polk returned home filled with confidence and ambition. As a sign of how he had grown, he asked his brothers and sisters not to call him Jim or Jimmy, but James.

James Polk was the kind of young man who could envision a goal and move toward it with careful planning. He wanted to go into politics, he was sure of that. The most direct path to that career was to study law. He was fortunate to train in the Nashville offices of Felix Grundy, a very successful, self-educated lawyer with a gift for gab. The two would remain friends, colleagues, and sometimes friendly rivals for many years.

In 1819, Grundy was elected to the Tennessee state legislature. One hot summer day, he returned to his office and suggested that another law student apply for the clerkship of the state senate, which met for a few weeks each year in Murfreesboro, then the state capital. The young man turned down the suggestion. James overheard the conversation and approached his fellow apprentice. "As you have refused Mr. Grundy's offer," Polk said, "I would be glad if you would tell him that I would like to have the place myself." With Grundy's help, James became senate clerk.

For the next four years, James traveled from Nashville to Murfreesboro to act as clerk when the state senate was in session there. The clerkship was an excellent perch from which to observe government and politicians at work. James was responsible for taking notes on senate actions, and for moving bills and other business through the *legislative* (lawmaking) process. During four years on the job, he also got to know some of the top leaders in the state.

While serving as clerk, James also completed his studies and qualified to practice law in 1820. His real aim, however, was to run for public office. In 1823, he announced that he would run for the seat in the state legislature representing Maury County, his family's home county.

Polk's opponent was William Yancey, who already held the office. James had never run a campaign before, but he saw a way to defeat his older, more experienced opponent. He traveled endless miles on horseback to introduce himself to voters in the district and to make stump speeches. (They were often delivered using the flat stump of a tree as a platform.) In the days before radio and television, a political campaign was an entertainment, and audiences greeted candidates with enthusiasm.

The election was held during two days in the summer of 1823. Polling places were like loud parties. Alcohol was supplied by the candidates. At one election district alone, Polk provided 23 gallons (87 liters) of hard cider, brandy, and whiskey. Fueled by the excitement of the occasion and by the drinks, men argued loudly about candidates and issues, and sometimes ended up fighting each other.

The vote was not taken by secret ballot. Each voter had to announce his choice out loud for all his neighbors to hear. The race seesawed between Polk and Yancey. In the end, James had captured his first election at the age of 27.

The following winter, James took another major step. On January 1, 1824, he married 20-year-old Sarah Childress. He had probably met Sarah in Murfreesboro when the state senate was in session. She was the daughter of a successful merchant and planter there, who made sure she received the best education possible for a girl at that time. "Her eyes looked as if she had a great deal of spice," commented one guest at the wedding.

The wedding was a huge social occasion, with dinners and parties continuing for several days. Through the years, James and Sarah would prove true friends, and partners in furthering James's career.

An early portrait of Sarah Childress Polk.

In the legislature, Polk set out as a leading reformer, working to change laws to help the poor. He battled for debt relief (in those days, men who could not pay their debts could be sent to prison), for bank reform, and for creation of a public school system in Tennessee. Although he did not always win, his effectiveness caught the attention of powerful politicians—including one of the great leaders in U.S. history.

From Tennessee to D.C.

When Andrew Jackson emerged as a powerful political force in the early 1820s, James strongly supported him. In 1823, Polk helped Jackson get elected to the U.S. Senate. In 1824, he supported the general's failed run for the presidency. In return, Jackson supported Polk for Tennessee's sixth district seat in the U.S. House of Representatives in 1825. Polk's opponent for the district seat was Andrew Erwin. Erwin was a bitter opponent of Jackson, who had killed Erwin's son-in-law in a duel. To make matters more difficult for Polk, other pro-Jackson men also decided to run, taking likely votes away from Polk.

Still, with Jackson's support and his own hard work, James won the election. Out of 10,000 votes cast, Polk received 3,669 and Erwin 2,748, with many other candidates splitting the rest. One of Polk's friends wrote that the election was decided by Polk's personal popularity and "earnestness and sincerity of manner."

Andrew Jackson (born 1767–died 1845) was a bigger-than-life American character. Born in the Carolinas nearly 30 years before James Polk, he was orphaned at an early age, but managed to study law, and moved west to present-day Tennessee as a young man. In 1796, he became the state's first congressman in the U.S. House of Representatives.

Andrew Jackson, a friend of James Polk's father and a main sponsor of James Polk's political career.

Jackson became a leading figure in Nashville. He built a prosperous plantation, served as a judge, and commanded local militia in times of trouble. He also gained a reputation for his dangerous temper. He killed one man in a duel and was twice wounded himself in private gunfights.

During the War of 1812, Jackson's military exploits made him a national hero. In 1814, he decisively defeated Creek warriors, allies of the British, in Alabama. Then in January 1815, he drove away a British force that was attacking New Orleans. His men called him "Old Hickory" because his toughness reminded them of that hardwood tree.

Jackson was chosen to represent Tennessee in the U.S. Senate in 1823. The next year, he ran for president, but lost a disputed election to John Quincy Adams. Jackson would win the presidency decisively in 1828 and 1832, and become the most powerful political leader of the era.

Andrew Jackson was a longtime friend of James Polk's father and probably knew James when he was a boy. Because he never had any children of his own, Jackson often took special interest in the careers of his young supporters. He became James Polk's mentor and friend. More than anyone, he was responsible for Polk's rise in politics.

☆ ☆ ☆

The U.S. Capitol as it looked when Polk first came to Washington, D.C. Cows are grazing in the foreground. The Capitol has been greatly enlarged since Polk's time.

When he reached Washington to take up his new duties, James had just turned 30. His political philosophy was fairly well set. He was a "Jeffersonian"—a believer in Thomas Jefferson's ideas about government. In general, he thought that the *federal*, or national, government should keep its nose out of the business of individual states. Polk also believed that the federal government should stay as small as possible. Its main purposes should be to defend the United States and deal with relations with other countries. He favored low *tariffs*—taxes on goods *imported* (brought in) from other countries. Finally, he believed that the federal government should not pay for internal improvements such as roads or canals, leaving such improvements to the states and to private business.

John Quincy Adams, who became president in 1825, disagreed with most of Polk's beliefs. He thought the federal government should do more to help improve roads, canals, and schools nationwide. In an 1827 speech, Polk said that Adams's proposed national projects "all mark the departure from that republican simplicity and purity in which . . . Jefferson administered the Government."

In 1827, Polk was reelected to his House seat, and Jackson supporters gained a *majority*—more than half the votes—in both the House and the Senate. Now Polk and his allies could frustrate the plans of John Quincy Adams and could help plan for Andrew Jackson's election to the presidency in 1828.

John Quincy Adams, who was president when Polk entered Congress. Adams defeated Polk's hero Andrew Jackson in a disputed election in 1824–25.

In the midst of these exciting plans, Polk faced personal sorrow. His father, who had always been there to help James with financial and fatherly support, died in the fall of 1827. His death set off arguments among the Polk brothers and sisters about who would inherit what. As the eldest son, James had to referee the family arguments.

The 1828 presidential election was a grudge match. Jackson bitterly insisted that Adams had "stolen" the 1824 election from him, and he was determined to win it this time. Polk provided valuable advice during the campaign, even though he was nearly 30 years younger than the general. Polk's cautious and thoughtful manner helped balance Jackson's hotheaded approach.

Adams was an unpopular president, and Jackson's popularity had increased since 1824. In the 1828 rematch, Jackson won a smashing victory and became the seventh president of the United States. He promised to return the federal government to all the people and to challenge the power of rich merchants, bankers, and landowners. On the day he took office in March 1829, Jackson invited all citizens to a reception at the White House. Thousands came to congratulate him. In their enthusiasm, they broke furniture and spilled food and drink. When the crowds nearly crushed Jackson himself, the party was moved outside to the White House lawn.

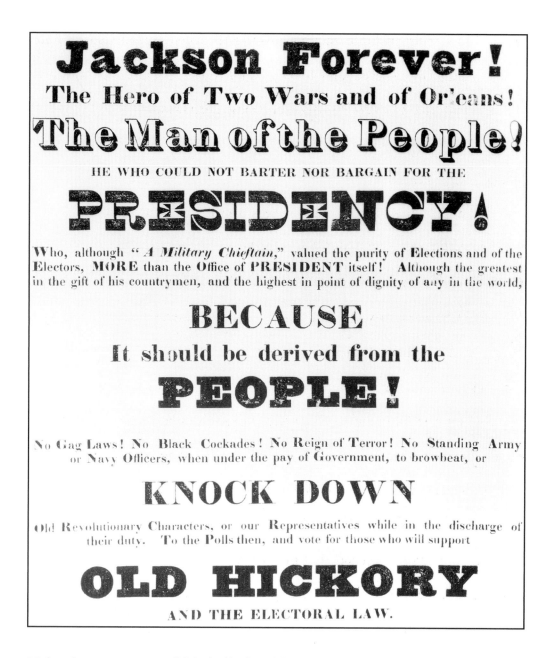

A Jackson election poster in 1828. Polk helped "Old Hickory" defeat John Quincy Adams and go to the White House.

Notes from Abroad

After 1820, Europeans developed a strong curiosity about the growing young country across the Atlantic. Many European travelers visited the United States and later published their impressions about Americans. Here are excerpts from the writings of two such tourists—Frances Trollope of Great Britain, and Alexis de Tocqueville of France.

Frances Trollope

[I noticed the Americans'] total want of all the usual courtesies of the table, the voracious rapidity with which the [food was] seized and devoured . . . the loathsome spitting, from the contamination of which it was absolutely impossible to protect our dresses; the frightful manner of feeding with their knives, till the whole blade seemed to enter the mouth; and the still more frightful manner of cleaning the teeth afterwards with a pocket knife.

Alexis de Tocqueville

In Europe we are wont [have a tendency] to look upon a restless disposition, an unbounded desire for riches, and an excessive love of independence as propensities very dangerous to society. Yet these are the very elements that ensure a long and peaceful future to the republics of America. . . . What we should call cupidity [greed], the Americans frequently term a laudable industry [good hard work], and they blame as faint-heartedness what we consider to be the virtue of moderate desires.

★ ★ ★

Jackson's Man in the House ——————

After Jackson took office in 1829, James Polk became one of his main leaders in the House of Representatives. When Polk ran for reelection in Tennessee in 1829 and 1831, he was so popular that no other candidates ran against him.

One of Polk's main tasks in the House was to help pass a new tariff bill to replace the hated high tariffs passed during the presidency of John Quincy Adams. Northern manufacturers wanted high tariffs, because tariffs made foreign goods more expensive. This encouraged people to buy American goods instead. Southerners hated high tariffs. They sold most of their cotton in Britain and bought British goods with the money. The tariffs made those goods wildly expensive, and southern planters felt they were paying the tariffs out of their own pockets. Polk understood the planters' point of view. In 1829, he told voters, "It must ever be unjust to tax the labor of one class of society to support and fatten another."

Polk and his colleagues did pass a new tariff bill, but it did not lower the hated tax enough to please the leaders in the southern states. In 1832, John C. Calhoun, a leader of the southern forces and Jackson's vice president, resigned in disgust. He began supporting the idea that a state could refuse to obey a law it considered *unconstitutional*—not permitted by the U.S. Constitution. Encouraged

James K. Polk about 1829.

by Calhoun, the South Carolina legislature declared the federal tariffs "null and void" in their state. This idea of *nullification*—that a state could refuse to obey or enforce a federal law—threatened to break the power of the federal government. What if each state could pick and choose to obey only those federal laws it felt were fair?

President Jackson announced that nullification of a federal law by a state was an act of treason. If South Carolina refused to collect federal tariffs on goods from foreign countries, he would send in federal troops. With Polk's support, Jackson sent a bill to Congress authorizing the use of federal troops if necessary.

At the same time, the leaders of Congress worked feverishly to create a *compromise*—a new tariff act that angry southerners could agree to. The tariff compromise was negotiated by two of Jackson's bitterest opponents, Senator Henry Clay, who had been secretary of state under Adams, and former vice president John C. Calhoun. The Clay-Calhoun tariff bill offered a carrot (gradually decreasing tariffs), and Jackson's military bill threatened the stick (military action). Together, they succeeded in persuading South Carolina to back down, ending the nullification crisis.

James Polk was also facing crises in his private life. In 1831, three of his brothers died. James stepped in to help care for and support his brothers' children and wives as well as his own younger brothers and sisters, who still lived with

John C. Calhoun, who resigned as Jackson's vice president and encouraged his state of South Carolina to "nullify" a federal tariff law.

their mother. As the oldest surviving man in the family, James would have important family responsibilities for the rest of his life.

It was becoming clear that James and Sarah would have no children of their own, a serious disappointment to both of them. Sarah, though, was not the kind of person to fold up in the face of bad news. Without the responsibilities of raising children and managing a large household, she threw herself into her husband's career, becoming an expert on politics. When the House met, Sarah Polk was often in the ladies' gallery, watching James and his colleagues at work. Her keen observations and insights gave James an advantage in the political tangles he was now facing.

The nullification crisis was soon overshadowed by a bigger fight: President Jackson against the second Bank of the United States. Polk's role in this titanic struggle between a powerful president and powerful businessmen and bankers vaulted him into the national spotlight.

Chapter 3

How to Kill a Bank

According to a famous story, President Andrew Jackson was lying sick in bed when a visitor came to discuss current issues. When the subject of the bank came up, Jackson sat up in bed. "The bank thinks it will kill me," he coughed. "But I will kill it!"

The second Bank of the United States had been chartered by the federal government in 1816. It was organized to help regulate U.S. business by controlling the supply of money and giving guidance to smaller banks. The federal government agreed to keep its own funds in the bank.

Andrew Jackson was a longtime critic of the bank. He believed it had grown too powerful. Its directors were all private bankers who were not elected or appointed by the government. Jackson believed that the directors had become a tool of wealthy businessmen and merchants—at the expense of the common people. The government, Jackson said, should "confine itself to equal protection, and, as Heaven does its rains, shower its favors alike on the high and the low, the rich and the poor."

Bank supporters also had strong arguments. If the bank went out of business, they said, no one would control the currency. If too much was issued, inflation would send prices soaring. If too little was issued, other banks and businesses would not be able to borrow money and would soon be bankrupt.

Jackson was determined to bring the bank under control. The bank's president, Nicholas Biddle, was just as determined to force Jackson to live with the bank and its policies. The showdown came in 1832–33, with one politician calling it "one of the greatest struggles between democracy and the money power."

In 1832, Jackson's opponents decided to test him on the bank. It was a presidential election year, and Henry Clay of Kentucky thought he could destroy Jackson's popularity, using the bank issue as his weapon. That summer, Clay and Biddle presented the bank's charter for renewal (even though its current charter would not expire for four more years). Congress voted in favor of renewing the charter and sent it to Jackson to sign into law. If Jackson signed the bill, he would lose many of his supporters, who also hated the bank. If he *vetoed* the bill—

Nicholas Biddle, director of the second Bank of the United States and an enemy of Andrew Jackson's administration. Polk helped close down the bank.

refused to sign it and sent it back to Congress—Clay would accuse him of being a dictator who refused to approve a lawful vote by Congress.

Jackson not only vetoed the bill, he sent it back to Congress with a fiery message, explaining just why he opposed the second Bank of the United States. His message was a declaration of war on the bank. In order to pass the bill over the president's veto, Congress needed to pass it by two-thirds majorities in both the House and the Senate. Henry Clay and his allies did not have the votes, and the bank's charter was not renewed. Clay accused Jackson of being a dictator, just as he had planned. In November, however, the voters rallied around Jackson and he was easily reelected.

Biddle and bank supporters still hoped to defeat Jackson and save the bank. But Polk proved their match, opposing every move of the bank supporters to renew the charter. As chairman of the powerful House Ways and Means Committee, he took on the task of investigating the bank.

While Jackson's fiery temper and fierce opposition had knocked the bank off its feet, now Polk's cool head and research pinned it. His investigation revealed ways the bank had mismanaged business, lied about its operations, and used its money to help supporters and attack opponents. The bank "has set itself up as a great irresponsible rival power of the Government," Polk said. Support for the bank began to fade.

In 1833, President Jackson ordered the government to transfer its millions of dollars out of the national bank. Taking out such huge sums of federal money put a stake through the bank's heart. By 1836, the second Bank of the United States was dead.

Later, in a speech in Tennessee, President Jackson singled out his faithful ally. "Polk, for the hard service done in the cause [to kill the bank], deserves a medal from the American people," he said.

In this cartoon, President Jackson is destroying the national bank, and his opponents are trying to escape.

Mr. Speaker

In late December 1835, Polk was elected Speaker of the House. The Speaker is chosen by the majority party in the House and holds one of the most powerful posts in Washington, appointing the members of all House committees, presiding over debate and other business on the House floor, and making judgments about House rules. Sitting behind a large desk facing the members, the Speaker is essentially the president of the House.

With his usual hard work, Polk quickly mastered his new responsibilities. At the same time, it proved a great challenge for him, testing his brains, patience, even his bravery. Speaker Polk immediately became a target of attacks because of his close connection to President Jackson. Opponents charged that he was Jackson's puppet, willing to do anything to benefit the Jackson administration and the Democrats. As rivalry between the Democrats and the new anti-Jackson Whig party heated up, Polk was a target of criticism and abuse.

At first, foes like Virginia representative Henry A. Wise tried to embarrass him by asking tough questions about House rules. But the new speaker had done his homework and calmly provided the answers. Later, the insults grew more personal. After one angry session, an enraged Wise stuck a finger in the Speaker's chest and called him a "petty tyrant . . . I mean it personal!" Polk's friends were

The old House of Representatives chamber where James Polk presided as Speaker of the House from the raised desk in the center.

afraid that Wise—who was an expert marksman—was trying to draw James into a duel and kill him.

Polk never rose to the bait. Unlike Andrew Jackson, he preferred to sidestep an angry argument or fight. Throughout his career when debates grew hot, he had the discipline to stay cool.

The most serious issue Polk faced as Speaker was the growing division over slavery. Until the 1830s, most Americans—including Polk—had viewed slavery in the United States as an unavoidable evil. Many farmers and plantation owners in the South relied on slave labor to grow their tobacco, cotton, and other crops. Southern lawmakers argued that the Constitution gave the federal government no right to interfere with slavery.

Now, especially in the New England states, where slavery was banned, a movement was growing to abolish, or end, slavery once and for all. The *abolitionists*, as they were called, passionately argued that all slavery was immoral. Abolitionist members of the House presented petitions and draft bills on the floor of the House, where they sparked anger and insults from southern supporters of slavery. Often Polk had to interrupt debates to keep them from turning into shouting matches and fistfights.

The controversy threatened to stall House actions on any other issue. Finally, one member proposed a rule that would automatically table, or forbid debate on, any bill or petition about slavery. Polk and the Democrats managed to pass the rule over strong objections from the antislavery members in 1836. This so-called gag rule was renewed in each new session of the House until 1844.

In the meantime, things were not going well for the country or the Democratic Party. Democrat Martin Van Buren had been elected president in 1836, but months after he took office a great financial panic swept the country. Banks closed, merchants and farmers declared bankruptcy, and thousands in

Polk and Slavery

James K. Polk grew up in a slaveholding family, and he later owned and traded slaves himself. He personally thought that slavery was a wicked tradition. But like many Americans of his time, he also believed that slavery was necessary to the economy of the South and that the right to own slaves was protected by the U.S. Constitution.

It is uncertain how many slaves Polk owned, but we do know that they worked on his plantations in Tennessee and Mississippi and in his home. Polk fired several overseers who he felt were too cruel, and praised another who was fairer. "I am glad [this overseer] feeds well, clothes well, and is humane and attentive to the comfort of the [slaves]," he wrote in a letter.

However compassionate he may have been, Polk, like other slaveholders, profited from the sweat and toil of his human property.

☆★☆

An engraving of James K. Polk.

eastern cities rioted against higher food prices caused by inflation. The Whig party blamed Van Buren and the Democrats for the financial troubles and succeeded in electing Whigs. Even in Tennessee, the Whigs had elected a governor and majorities in the state legislature.

In 1839, Polk left his seat in the House of Representatives after 14 years, including four years as speaker. He had agreed to run for governor of Tennessee to break the growing power of the Whigs in his home state. Although Polk had endured a stormy term as Speaker, he was cheered by a letter from another House member: "While you were Speaker, your friends praised, and your enemies abused you, but it is now admitted, on all sides that James K. Polk was the best that we have had for many years, and some say—the best we ever had."

Racing Back Home

James Polk returned to Tennessee as one of the most powerful Democrats in the country. He faced a tough contest, though, against Whig governor Newton Cannon, who was running for reelection. Once again, Polk turned on his intense political energy. In the first two months of campaigning, he covered more than 1,300 miles (2,100 km) on horseback. He delivered 43 scheduled public addresses and many more unplanned ones. At first, Cannon tried to keep up, but

Polk campaigns in Tennessee from a makeshift platform to a crowd gathered on a hillside.

candidate Polk seemed tireless. "Polk has ten times the activity of Cannon," complained one Cannon supporter.

In the end, Polk won. He was just as pleased by the success of the state's other Democratic candidates. Whigs had to shake their heads and give James Polk credit for helping revive the Tennessee Democratic party.

Party! When Whigs Were Popular

After Andrew Jackson won his second presidential term in 1832, a new party emerged to do battle with the popular president—the Whigs. The name came from a British political party that opposed the powers of the British monarchy. The new U.S. party adopted the name because it believed it was also opposing a tyrant—President Jackson, whom they called "King Andrew the First."

The Whigs drew most of their strength from eastern businessmen, western farmers, and southern plantation owners. They believed in a stronger national government that would fund major improvements in the states. They also opposed President Jackson's attacks on the second Bank of the United States.

In 1840, the Whigs nominated General William Henry Harrison for president and John Tyler for vice president. After a campaign filled with songs and slogans, they defeated Democrat Martin Van Buren, putting a Whig in the presidency for the first time. The Whigs would elect only one more president. In the 1850s, torn apart by disagreements on slavery, the party fell apart. Northern Whigs, including an Illinois lawyer named Abraham Lincoln, joined the newly created Republican party.

☆ ☆ ☆

Polk, however, did not enjoy much success as governor. State lawmakers blocked most of his plans. He did succeed in opening a "lunatic asylum" (an early hospital for the mentally ill) and improving the state's public schools. "No people who are not [educated] can long remain free," he told voters.

In 1840, Polk explored running for vice president in President Martin Van Buren's run for reelection. Polk was lucky not to run with Van Buren, who was badly beaten by Whig candidate William Henry Harrison.

Governor Polk ran for reelection in 1841. This time, the Whigs found a candidate who could keep up with him—James Jones. Jones was over six feet (1.8 m) tall, but weighed only 125 pounds (57 kg), earning him the nickname "Lean Jimmy." The two traveled together giving "speakings"—speeches and debates—around the state.

Polk was 13 years older than Jones and much better qualified, but Jones proved to be a much more entertaining speaker. The Whigs also offered parades, music, and food and drink to entertain and befriend the voters. Polk tried to poke fun at his younger, inexperienced, goofy opponent, but this strategy often backfired. Jones kept his good humor, while Polk came across as mean.

In one talk, Polk joked that Jones was more suited to be a circus clown than governor of Tennessee. Jones grinned and shot back that both he and Polk would excel as circus performers, Jones as a clown and Polk as "the little fellow [a monkey] that is dressed in a red cap and jacket and who rides around on a pony." The audience burst into laughter and applause.

Polk's reasoned arguments could not compete with Jones's showmanship. Jones won, handing Polk his first-ever election loss. Two years later, Polk again ran against Jones for governor. Polk said that this election would "be decided by an appeal to reason and not by flags and fiddling." Tennessee voters disappointed him, reelecting Jones to a second term.

Whig newspapers had been predicting the end of Polk's political career ever since he returned from Washington. Now he had to wonder if they were right.

Chapter 4

The "Dark Horse"

After suffering two demoralizing election defeats, James K. Polk began one of the biggest comebacks in the history of U.S. politics. To revive his career, he hoped to gain the Democratic party's *nomination*—become its candidate—for vice president in 1844.

That year, Democrats seemed set to nominate former president Martin Van Buren as their candidate for president. If Van Buren, a New Yorker, was chosen, Polk figured the party might want him as the vice president to help appeal to southern and western voters.

Many Democrats were not excited about Van Buren's candidacy, however. He had been elected president in 1836, but in 1840 he had lost the presidency to Whig William Henry Harrison. Then in April 1844, Van Buren took a position that angered many Democrats. He published a letter stating that he was against *annexing* Texas—making it part of the United States.

51

Former president Martin Van Buren, who was the favorite for the Democratic nomination in 1844.

The United States had bought the region of Texas as part of the Louisiana Purchase in 1803, but in 1819 it had ceded the land to Spain by treaty. When Mexico gained its independence from Spain, the region became part of Mexico. In the 1830s, thousands of settlers from the United States moved to Texas. In 1836, Texas rebelled against Mexico and declared itself an independent republic.

A year after that, Texas leaders asked to become part of the United States. The government was slow to take action on this request. Antislavery forces in the northern states opposed annexing the region because it would almost certainly become a large and powerful slave state. Many others opposed annexation because it would almost certainly cause a war with Mexico, which still did not accept Texas independence.

By 1844, however, public opinion was swinging strongly in favor of annexing Texas, and the move was supported by many Democratic leaders. Van Buren was out of step with his party. Retired president Andrew Jackson announced that he favored quick annexation of Texas, and Polk did the same.

In May 1844, a divided Democratic party convention in Baltimore, Maryland, prepared to nominate its candidate for president. According to the rules, the winner had to receive two-thirds of the votes. *Delegates*, the representatives from each state party, would vote (or *ballot*) over and over until one candidate received the required number. On the first ballot Van Buren got 146 out of 266 votes—more than half, but still 31 votes short of the 177 needed. This was the highest total he would receive.

More ballots followed, and Van Buren steadily lost votes. On the seventh ballot, Lewis Cass of Michigan, who favored annexation, got 114 votes to Van Buren's 104. But it seemed impossible that any candidate could get near the 177 votes needed. The convention was hopelessly deadlocked.

From out of nowhere came James K. Polk. A group of Polk supporters began to work behind the scenes to offer their man as a compromise candidate, one who favored annexation but was also respected by Van Buren supporters. The two sides considered Polk someone they could agree on, and the stalemate was broken. On the eighth ballot, Polk received only 44 votes—but support for him gained momentum. On the ninth ballot, he was chosen as the Democratic candidate for president.

It was the first time a major U.S. party had chosen a "dark horse" presidential candidate—a nominee who had not received much attention beforehand. When the result was announced, said a reporter, "every person in the room . . . rose from his seat: and such waving of handkerchiefs and cheering I never saw or heard before." Later, the Democrats chose George M. Dallas to be Polk's running mate.

What Is a Dark Horse?

The term dark horse comes from horse-racing slang in Britain. Owners of a fast horse sure to win races could not make much money betting on their horse because it was always a favorite to win. To make more money, they disguised the horse by dyeing it a darker color and entering it in a race under a different name. Then they bet on the unknown "dark horse" and won big money when it unexpectedly won the race.

☆ ★ ☆

The Campaign of 1844

Supporters gave Polk the nickname "Young Hickory"—the new leader of "Old Hickory" Andrew Jackson's party.

Whigs had a slogan of their own. "WHO IS JAMES K. POLK?" they asked on signs and handbills. Their own candidate, Henry Clay, was among the best-known political leaders in the nation. He had been Speaker of the House when Polk was still a teenager and later was a founder of the Whig party and a leader of the attacks on Andrew Jackson. Clay believed he could beat Polk easily. In fact, he said he wished "that [a Democratic candidate] more worthy of a contest with us had . . . been selected."

To Clay's dismay, Polk proved a more than worthy candidate. To gain the support of other presidential hopefuls, he promised if elected to serve only one

Whig Henry Clay had already run for president and lost in 1824 and 1832. Now in 1844, he was confident of being elected.

HENRY CLAY,
AND
A PROTECTIVE TARIFF.

NO ANNEXATION OF TEXAS!

COMMERCE.

MECHANIC ARTS

AGRICULTURE

PROTECTIVE POLICY

MANUFACTURES

INTERNAL IMPROVEMENTS

No Extension of Slavery!!

With Henry Clay
We'll win the day,
And Home Industry defend;
With Polk and Dallas
We'll to the gallows
Free Trade and Texas send.

A Clay campaign ribbon shows some of the Whig campaign pledges—a protective tariff, no annexation of Texas, and no extension of slavery.

term so other Democrats could run four years later. He pledged to follow through on his vow to annex Texas. He pledged fair tariffs for both North and South.

Clay, on the other hand, made mistakes. At first he came out against annexation of Texas. But when this whipped up a storm of criticism, he waffled—changing his opinion back and forth. This cost him votes. The Whigs also accepted support from people who wanted to limit voting rights of *immigrants*—foreign-born people who had come to the United States to live and become citizens. This backfired, and large majorities of these citizens voted for Polk and the Democrats.

Vice President George M. Dallas

George M. Dallas (born 1792–died 1864) was a Pennsylvanian picked as Polk's running mate to help win votes in Pennsylvania and other northern states. Polk and Dallas were never close, however. Against Dallas's advice, Polk appointed James Buchanan secretary of state. Dallas and Buchanan were bitter rivals in Pennsylvania politics. As Polk relied on Buchanan more and more, Dallas fell out of favor and rarely spoke with Polk. Dallas remained loyal to his president, however, especially on the subject of Texas. The city and county of Dallas, Texas, may have been named for him as a result.

☆ ☆ ☆

The "Grand Banner" for the Democratic ticket, with pictures of Polk and his vice-presidential running mate, George Dallas.

In November, as the votes were counted, Polk rested at his home in Columbia, Tennessee. Friends and supporters waited and worried with him. Worry turned to celebration, though, when results showed that Polk had won the election by a razor-thin margin, just over one percent of the popular vote. He won 170 electoral votes to Clay's 105.

In an amazing turnaround, James K. Polk had risen from political defeat to President of the United States in little more than a year.

"The Hardest-Working Man in America" ——

James K. Polk took office on March 4, 1845. At 49 years old, he was the youngest U.S. president until that time. Thousands of people came from around the country to attend the *inauguration*, the ceremony in which he would take the oath of office. However, a downpour turned the day into a soggy affair. Former president John Quincy Adams joked that the new president delivered his inaugural address to "a large assemblage of umbrellas."

In his address, Polk outlined his plans and hopes for his four-year term. He promised to keep government spending under control. He repeated his strong anti-Bank beliefs. He promised to keep the federal government from meddling too much in state affairs. He defended slavery, saying that those who sought to

Polk takes the oath of office on the steps of the Capitol in March 1845, as the crowd protects itself from the rain.

end it were trying to split the country. Finally, he vowed to push for the westward expansion of the United States.

"Who's James K. Polk?" his supporters shouted during the day's parades and parties, making fun of the Whigs' election slogan. "He's the president!" came the gleeful answer. Backers waved hickory tree branches to show their zeal for "Young Hickory." The new president, though, was a very different leader from "Old Hickory."

In appearance, James K. Polk had thin lips and high cheekbones beneath intense, gray eyes. He wore his gray hair long, sweeping it straight back where it curled over his collar. At five-foot-eight (1.73 m) and about 170 pounds (77 kg), he was not a big man. Concerned that no one would notice him when he came into a White House reception, his wife Sarah instructed musicians to play "Hail to the Chief" to signal Polk's entrance. That presidential tradition continues to this day.

Although respected by most colleagues and acquaintances, Polk was not well liked. He had no close friends besides his wife, Sarah. And even the relationship with his best friend, Cave Johnson, was built around politics and promoting Polk's career. President Polk was not fond of socializing, unless it served some political purpose. He relied on Sarah to organize entertainment and dinners at the White House. She proved an excellent hostess, supplying much of the charm her husband lacked. But James apparently did enjoy visits from his

A presidential portrait of James K. Polk.

nephews and nieces, some of whom stayed at the White House for weeks, months, and even years at a time.

The president had no hobbies, and read only newspapers, reports, and the Bible. For President Polk, it seemed that every waking moment was meant for work. "My time has been wholly occupied in my office, in the discharge of my public duties," he noted in his diary. "My confinement to my office has been constant & unceasing and my labours very great." Later in his presidency he boasted, "In truth, though I occupy a very high position, I am the hardest working man in this country."

The new president was all business. While this sober attitude did not make him popular or widely loved, it did help make him one of the most effective presidents in U.S. history.

Tariffs and the Treasury

Once he took office, Polk wasted no time in tackling four goals he had set for his presidency. One was to lower tariffs. These *taxes* provided most of the money used to run the federal government, but they were also used to make foreign goods more expensive and protect the business of American manufacturers. Southern planters believed that the high "protectionist" tariff was a tax on them, since many of the foreign goods they bought were taxed. Only twelve years earlier, South Carolina had refused to collect tariffs at all.

Headman of Horror

The hideous murder accomplished, I set myself forthwith . . . to the task of concealing the body. . . . At one period I thought of cutting the corpse into minute fragments, and destroying them by fire. At another, I resolved to dig a grave for it in the floor of the cellar . . .

—From "The Black Cat" by
Edgar Allan Poe

Writer of grim and mysterious stories and poems, Edgar Allan Poe.

Edgar Allan Poe (born 1809–died 1849) was America's first specialist of spooky and headman of horror. His stories, many published while Polk was president, created a sensation for their dark, often morbid, view of life. In *The Murders in the Rue Morgue*, Poe created a new kind of fiction—the "detective" story. His poetry includes "Annabel Lee," "The Bells," and others that American schoolchildren read and recited for more than a century. "The Raven," about a mysterious bird who speaks one word—"Nevermore"—became one of the most familiar poems in the English language.

☆★☆

Polk's secretary of the treasury, Robert J. Walker, studied the subject for months. He worked out a compromise bill that lowered tariffs on imports but still offered some protections to U.S. manufacturers. After much debate in Congress, the bill passed by narrow margins in both the Senate and the House. Few were completely happy with the result, of course, but the Walker Tariff Bill helped settle a controversial issue. Polk called it "vastly the most important domestic measure of my administration."

The creation of the "independent treasury" was another of Polk's goals. How to handle government funds had remained a big question since President Jackson's showdown with the national bank (see chapter 3). Partly as a result of Jackson's anti-Bank policies, the country had suffered a severe financial depression. Now Polk worked with Congress to pass the Independent Treasury Act of 1846, which gave the federal government some of the tools of the old national bank. The new system was effective, finally settling a long-running dispute.

However important these accomplishments were, they were overshadowed by Polk's other accomplishments. These had to do with territory—Texas, Oregon, and California. The president joined many Americans in believing that the United States was destined to expand its territory across North America. However, Polk also set the country marching toward war.

Chapter 5

Eye to Eye with Great Britain —————

In 1845, editor John L. O'Sullivan wrote that it was the country's "Manifest Destiny to overspread the continent allotted by Providence [God] for the free development of our yearly multiplying millions." The term *Manifest Destiny* suggests that it is God's will for the United States to expand across the continent. The phrase became the rallying cry of Americans who favored expansion. There were obstacles to overcome, however, including Great Britain and Mexico.

The United States and Great Britain agreed in 1818 to work together in the Oregon country and renewed their agreement in 1827. By 1845, however, a steady flow of American settlers were following the Oregon Trail to the fertile valleys in the far west. About 5,000 Americans had settled in Oregon, compared with only 700 settlers from British territories. The settlers—and many political leaders—began demanding that the region become a territory of the United States.

The United States and Great Britain had been in on-again off-again negotiations about the Oregon country's future for years. The British wanted the boundary between the United States and British Canada to be drawn at the Columbia River, the present-day boundary between Oregon and Washington states. The Americans wanted a boundary farther north, putting the valuable harbors of Puget Sound (near present-day Seattle, Washington) within U.S. boundaries. Neither side would give in.

In Polk's inaugural address, he said, "Our title to the country of Oregon is 'clear and unquestionable,' and already are our people preparing to perfect that title by occupying it with their wives and children." Those words landed in the offices of the British government like a bomb. Was the United States planning to grab that land? Was Polk willing to go to war for it?

The president hoped it would not come to that. Even so, he was determined to get his way. He suggested the United States wanted *all* of the Oregon country, clear to the 54°40' line of latitude. This would give the United States the Pacific shoreline from southern Oregon to the shores of Alaska (then claimed by Russia) and shut off British Canada's access to the Pacific. In taking this extreme position, Polk hoped to force the British to give up more land. "The only way to treat John Bull [a nickname for Great Britain] was to look him straight in the eye," he said later.

Great Britain, then the most powerful country in the world, did not blink. "We are sincerely and anxiously desirous of a peaceful [solution]," wrote a British official to President Polk. "But if you desire war, . . . you will have it."

Negotiations continued throughout 1845. Tensions ran high. Americans fell into two camps on the issue—one side was willing to settle for a border at the 49th parallel, but a growing number demanded all of the territory or war. They took up the slogan "54-40 or Fight!" Some pioneers even painted those words on their Oregon-bound wagons.

At times the two sides seemed near a settlement, at others they seemed close to war. Then in February 1846, word reached Washington that 30 British warships were preparing to sail for North America. At the same time, tensions were rising between the United States and Mexico along the Texas border. If war with Mexico broke out, Polk worried that he might be faced with two wars at the same time or that he might be forced to give in to the British. Some diplomats even worried that the British might team up with Mexico.

Just before the U.S.-Mexican War erupted, Britain and the United States came to agreement. The border was set at the 49th parallel, the line of latitude that already served as the border between the United States and Canada from the

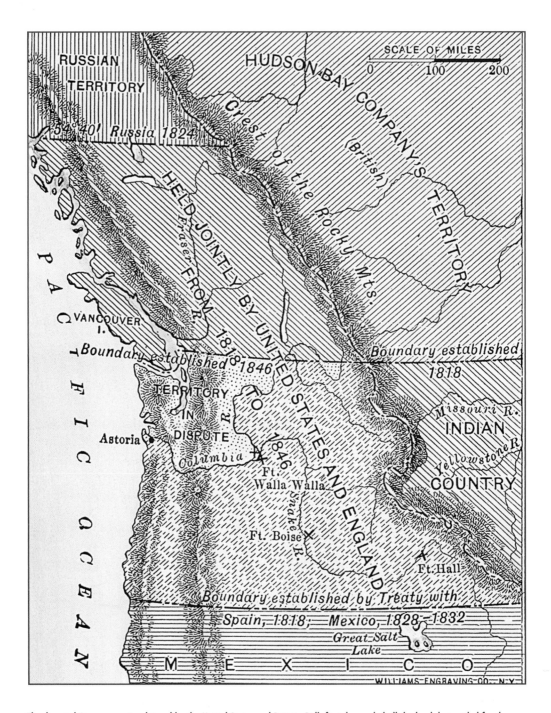

The disputed Oregon country claimed by the United States and Britain. Polk first demanded all the land, but settled for the land between the two lower lines—present-day states of Washington, Oregon, and Idaho and parts of Montana and Wyoming.

Great Lakes to the Rocky Mountains. Britain would occupy all lands north of that line, together with Vancouver Island (which dips slightly south of the 49th parallel) and would have permission to maintain a trading post on the Columbia River. The United States gained all of the territory south of that line. This "compromise" was the settlement that Polk had in mind to begin with. His aggressive demand for more territory helped bring the result he wanted.

Unlike Great Britain, though, Mexico was not in a negotiating mood.

Mexico and Texas

Polk got help on the annexation of Texas from an unlikely source—outgoing Whig president John Tyler. Vice President Tyler had taken over as president when William Henry Harrison died in 1841, and spent a miserable term in office. His *cabinet* (leaders of government departments) disagreed with his policies and resigned. Later, he was thrown out of his own Whig party after vetoing Whig bills establishing a new national bank. By 1844, it was clear that neither party would even consider nominating him for a full term.

Tyler did favor annexing Texas, however. Between the time Polk was elected in November 1844 and the time he took office in March 1845, Tyler helped push a bill through Congress to annex the new territory and signed the bill into law two days before he left office.

Polk completed the annexation details, and by December 1845, Texas had become the 27th state. It was clear, however, that there would be further complications. Mexico refused to accept the annexation and was threatening war. Polk seemed to want a war himself. The immediate issue was a dispute about the Texas-Mexico border.

The United States claimed that the border was the river called the Rio Grande. Mexico claimed that the border was the Nueces River, about 150 miles (240 km) farther to the north and east. Late in 1845, Polk sent U.S. troops to Corpus Christi, at the mouth of the Nueces. Then in March 1846, he instructed General Zachary Taylor to push into the disputed territory between the rivers and build a fort on the north bank of the Rio Grande. A Mexican force soon arrived on the south bank.

On April 24, 1846, Mexican general Mariano Arista sent a polite note to General Taylor: "Hostilities have commenced."

The next day, Mexican cavalry crossed the Rio Grande upriver from where General Taylor's men were building the fort. Taylor sent 65 mounted soldiers to scout the enemy movements. After a long ride, the Americans were caught by surprise and came under heavy fire. Eleven Americans were killed, and all the rest were captured.

The United States entered territory claimed by Mexico and Texas in early 1846 and built Fort Texas (at right) overlooking the Rio Grande. The Mexican town of Matamoros is across the river.

Two weeks later, news of the skirmish reached President Polk. He called an emergency meeting of his cabinet. On May 11, he asked Congress to declare war on Mexico, using the April 25 attack on U.S. troops as his reason. "Mexico has passed the boundary of the United States, has invaded our territory and shed American blood on the American soil. . . . the two nations are now at war." Congress passed the war resolution on May 13.

Polk's declaration was met with enthusiasm and "war fever" by many Americans. The president called for 50,000 volunteers to swell the small U.S. army for wartime—200,000 responded. Some states filled their quotas so quickly that eager young men had to move to other states to join up.

Not everyone was thrilled about the war. For U.S. troops to cross the disputed territory and build a fort on the Rio Grande, said one U.S. senator, was "as much an act of aggression on our part as is a man's pointing a pistol at another's breast." Years later, former president Ulysses S. Grant, who served as a young officer in the war, wrote that it was "one of the most unjust wars ever waged by a stronger against a weaker nation."

Polk had most of the country behind him, however, and he pushed ahead. However unfair his reasons for going to war, he proved to be a capable *commander in chief*. He came up with a two-pronged strategy. General Taylor was to invade Mexico across the Rio Grande. A second force was sent west to attack Mexican forts at Santa Fe (in present-day New Mexico) and proceed to Upper California (the present-day state of California).

Zachary Taylor proved an able general. After defeating Mexican forces north of the Rio Grande, he crossed the river and captured the Mexican city of Monterrey. Early in 1847, Mexico sent its army to destroy Taylor's forces. Greatly outnumbered, Taylor moved his troops to rugged territory at Buena Vista ranch. There, in February 1847, he fought off the much larger Mexican force and forced it to retreat, leaving the Rio Grande and much of northern Mexico in American hands. Even though it was often outnumbered, Taylor's army had much better weapons, equipment, supplies, and training than the Mexican forces.

Polk and his advisers expected Mexico to see that it was outmatched and to surrender in a matter of weeks. He had already set the terms that he would

Fast Facts
THE U.S.-MEXICAN WAR

Who: The U.S. against Mexico

When: May 1846 through February 1848

Why: Simmering tensions, the 1845 U.S. annexation of Texas, and a border dispute sparked fighting. The U.S. also wanted huge sections of Mexican territory.

Where: U.S. troops drove Mexican forces out of disputed territory in Texas; captured Monterrey in northern Mexico; captured lands in present-day New Mexico, Arizona, and California; besieged and captured Veracruz and Mexico City in Mexico.

Outcome: With the signing of the Treaty of Guadalupe Hidalgo in 1848, the U.S. gained undisputed claim to Texas; all of present-day California, Nevada, and Utah; most of New Mexico and Arizona; and parts of Colorado, Wyoming, Kansas, and Oklahoma.

Interesting Fact: Of about 13,800 U.S. soldiers who died during the war, only 1,700 died from battle wounds. Most died of disease.

Weapons of the U.S.-Mexican War

Like all wars, the U.S.-Mexican conflict was a testing ground for new weapons. The U.S. military introduced new and improved armaments, while the Mexican army had mostly old-fashioned weapons. This gave the United States a big advantage on the battlefield.

The recently developed Colt revolver was one of the U.S. Army's superior weapons that helped defeat Mexico in the war.

Most soldiers on both sides still carried muskets into battle, but some Americans were armed with rifles. A rifle has a spiral groove cut inside its barrel, which gives spin to the bullet when fired. Rifles are much more accurate and can be used over longer distances. The war also saw the first military use of the Colt revolver. Unlike the one-shot flintlock pistol, the revolver could fire several rounds without reloading.

The biggest difference was the Americans' new artillery. A U.S. officer named Sam Ringgold revolutionized the weaponry before he was killed early in the war. He put lighter cannons on fast-moving gun carriages so that they could be positioned quickly. Then he drilled his gunners constantly until they could reload and fire their weapons every ten seconds. The heavier, clumsy Mexican cannons could not compete.

★☆☆

demand for ending the war. But Santa Anna—the Mexican general and political leader—was determined to keep up the fight. Meanwhile, support for the war in the United States was already shrinking. The president's political opponents began calling it "Mr. Polk's War."

Polk knew he needed decisive action. Soon after Taylor's victory at Buena Vista, an American army of 10,000 men under General Winfield Scott sailed across the Gulf of Mexico to Veracruz, Mexico, far to the south. By the end of March 1847, it captured Veracruz and began marching inland toward Mexico City, the country's capital. Santa Anna and the Mexican army tried to stop the new invasion at the battle of Cerro Gordo. Scott outfoxed Santa Anna's troops by sending part of his army across a mountainous area the Mexicans thought impassable. These Americans surprised the Mexicans and chased them from the battlefield. Now nothing stood between the U.S. Army and Mexico City.

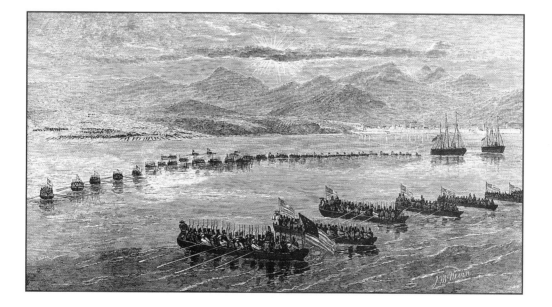

U.S. troops in a huge flotilla of landing craft approach Veracruz, Mexico, in 1847. After a siege, they captured the city, then began their march inland toward the Mexican capital.

In September 1847, General Scott's army triumphantly enters the main plaza in Mexico City after Mexican troops have surrendered.

By August, the bulk of Scott's troops were at the outskirts of the Mexican capital. On September 13, U.S. soldiers slammed home the victory by capturing the Castle of Chapultepec in some of the war's bloodiest fighting. The city surrendered the next day. The fighting was over, but negotiations dragged on until February 2, 1848, when the two countries finally signed the Treaty of Guadalupe Hidalgo.

Mexico surrendered more than 500,000 square miles (1.3 million km^2)— half of its territory. It gave up all claim to Texas to the Rio Grande border and ceded its territories of New Mexico and Upper California. The region includes most of present-day Arizona and New Mexico; all of California, Nevada, and Utah; and parts of four other present-day states. In return, the United States paid Mexico $15 million and agreed to pay some Mexican debts. President Polk had turned Manifest Destiny into reality.

President Polk's Last Months

Having spread U.S. territory from the Atlantic to the Pacific Oceans, Polk had achieved all his presidential goals. He hoped these successes might unite the country in national spirit, but in this he was sadly disappointed.

Even as the country expanded, the issue of slavery still threatened to rip the country apart. In fact, the new lands brought up the most difficult question: would new territories and states be slave states or free states? Even many moderates who agreed that slavery should be allowed to continue in the South believed that slavery should not be allowed to spread throughout the West. Polk's solution was to leave "the question of slavery . . . to the people of the new States when they came to form a State constitution for themselves." The idea was opposed by abolitionists and southern proslavery activists alike. Polk discovered that there was not much middle ground left between the two sides.

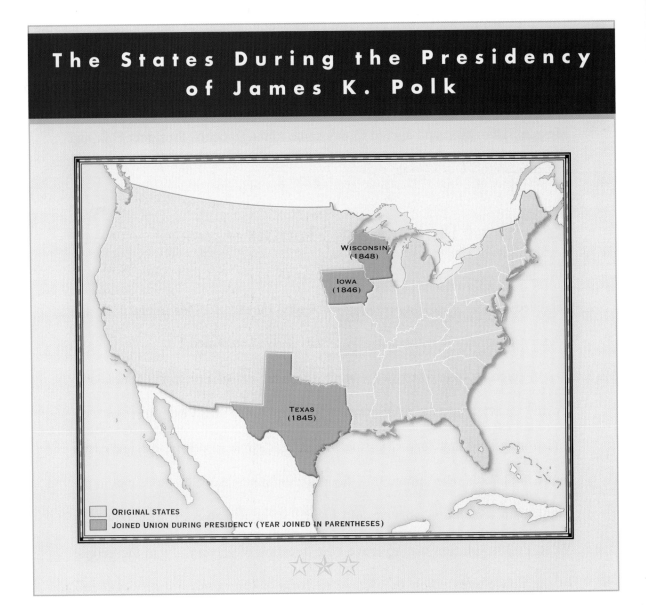

The States During the Presidency of James K. Polk

WISCONSIN
(1848)

IOWA
(1846)

TEXAS
(1845)

ORIGINAL STATES

JOINED UNION DURING PRESIDENCY (YEAR JOINED IN PARENTHESES)

☆ ☆ ☆

In 1848, his last full year as president, Polk addressed several other subjects. He offered to buy Cuba, just 90 miles (145 km) off the coast of Florida, from Spain, but Spain refused the offer. On July 4, he laid the cornerstone for the Washington Monument. It would one day rise majestically above Washington, D.C., but would not be completed for 40 years. In his annual message to Congress, Polk announced that his administration had almost finished the long task of moving Native Americans from lands east of the Mississippi River, opening 18.5 million acres (7.4 million ha) "for settlement and cultivation."

Democratic supporters begged Polk to run again in 1848, but he kept his promise to serve only one term. The Democrats nominated Lewis Cass, most recently senator from Michigan. Cass lost the support of antislavery Democrats, however. They formed a third party and ran former president Martin Van Buren. This allowed the election of Whig candidate Zachary Taylor—one of the heroes of the Mexican War. Polk thought Taylor "a well meaning old man. He is, however, uneducated, exceedingly ignorant of public affairs, and . . . of very ordinary capacity [ability]."

Polk's term concluded in March 1849, and the president was not sorry to see it end. "I am sure I shall be happier in my retirement than I have been during the four years I have filled the highest office," he wrote. Polk was only 53, but the job had worn him down. "In the brief period of four years," commented Secretary of State James Buchanan, "[Polk] has assumed the appearance of an old man."

First Lady Sarah Childress Polk

Sarah Childress Polk (born 1803–died 1891) was her husband's closest confidante and political adviser. "None but Sarah," the president said, "knew so intimately my private affairs." Raised in a wealthy Tennessee family, Sarah was used to the finer things in life. She dressed elegantly, and had striking dark eyes and hair.

In an age when women were expected to care only about their families, Sarah had been well educated and was very shrewd about politics. She served as her husband's unofficial secretary, and helped keep him up to date, reviewing magazine and newspaper articles and clipping the most important for him to read.

As first lady, Sarah was famed for charming both friends and political foes alike. One Whig who had often argued with the president said about Sarah, "her sweetness of manner won me entirely." She proved a gifted hostess for the many official dinners and parties. She was also a devoted churchgoer. She refused to serve whiskey or other hard liquor in the White House and did not allow dancing at White House functions.

In some ways, James and Sarah Polk were on very formal terms. When he was away and wrote to her, he always signed his letters "James K. Polk." Yet Sarah's devotion continued even after his death. For the rest of her life—42 years—she wore black mourning clothes.

☆ ★ ☆

Sarah Childress Polk.

Zachary Taylor, hero of the U.S.-Mexican War and Whig candidate for president in 1848. He defeated Democratic candidate Lewis Cass and took office in March 1849.

Characteristically, Polk worked until sundown on his last full day in office. "I disposed of all business on my table down to the minutest [smallest] detail and at the close of the day left a clean table for my successor."

After Taylor's inauguration, James and Sarah did make a triumphant tour of southern states. Everywhere they went, the ex-president was met by cheering crowds and tributes. Then in New Orleans, he fell ill. Terrible digestive pain and diarrhea plagued him all the way back to Tennessee. Arriving home in April, he improved in the familiar surroundings. "I am again at my home, in the midst of the friends of my youth," he said. "Henceforth I shall be a private citizen."

Unfortunately, James and Sarah did not have long to enjoy their new-found private lives. In June, Polk's condition worsened. He died on June 15, 1849, only 103 days after leaving office. With his passing, James Polk left behind a United States he had done so much to expand, but also a country very unsure of its future.

Chapter 6

Power to the President

James K. Polk may have been the hardest-working president to ever hold the office. Judging from his presidential diaries, he also had supreme self-confidence. He never doubted that the decisions he made were the correct ones, and he constantly watched over the shoulders of his cabinet members.

More than earlier presidents, Polk demonstrated how a president can influence the making of new laws. According to the Constitution, only Congress has the power to create legislation. Polk found ways to influence Congress to pass legislation he favored. Like Andrew Jackson, Polk saw himself as the sole representative of everyone in the United States. "The President represents . . . the whole people of the United States as each member of the legislative branch represents portions of them," he said in a speech. He proposed his own legislative program, then worked to convince federal lawmakers to turn it into law. He also appealed to the public to pressure their representatives to agree with his ideas. This approach helped push through the tariff bill of 1846 and led to the creation of an independent treasury.

Polk also used another way to control Congress's actions—the veto. In 1846, for example, Congress passed an "internal improvements" bill. This legislation was designed to pay for projects to better harbors and rivers. Polk vetoed the bill, arguing that the Constitution did not allow the federal government the right to fund such projects. He also believed that such a law would start a dishonest "scramble for the public money" by politicians. Congress tried but failed to override Polk's veto.

Besides expanding presidential influence over new laws, Polk also proved a strong commander in chief of the U.S. military. The Constitution gives Congress the power to declare war, but the president is in charge of the country's military forces. Polk was the first U.S. president to lead the country during a war fought mainly on foreign soil. Although he had little military training himself, he hired and fired generals, made sure the army had the men and supplies it needed, and planned strategy—where and how to attack. His leadership helped win a decisive victory over Mexico, and set an example for future wartime presidents to follow.

A photograph of Polk shows that he grew his hair long in the back. Later pictures of him, done after long hair went out of style, show him with shorter hair.

Polk also strengthened the training and preparatation of U.S. military forces. His administration helped create the U.S. Naval Academy in Annapolis, Maryland, in 1845. The academy has provided superior training to naval officers ever since. Actual combat during the U.S.-Mexican War also helped train and season the military forces. Tragically, many of the officers who fought against Mexico would fight each other only 14 years later in the U.S. Civil War. Among the veterans of the Mexican war were Union generals Ulysses S. Grant and George B. McClellan, and Confederate generals Robert E. Lee, Thomas "Stonewall" Jackson, and P. G. T. Beauregard.

From Sea to Shining Sea

In President Polk's last annual message to Congress, he listed ways the U.S. map had changed during his administration: "Within less than four years the annexation of Texas to the Union has been [completed]; all conflicting title to the Oregon Territory . . . has been adjusted, and New Mexico and . . . California have been acquired by treaty."

Polk saw these additions of land as his greatest contribution to the country—nearly 1.2 million square miles (3.1 million km^2). He used aggressive diplomacy with Great Britain to add the Oregon region south of the 49th parallel. He gained the vast American Southwest through an aggressive war against Mexico.

Although many questioned the way Polk provoked Mexico, few have questioned Polk's management of the war once it began, or the importance of its results. His war and diplomacy added the last big pieces to the map of the continental United States.

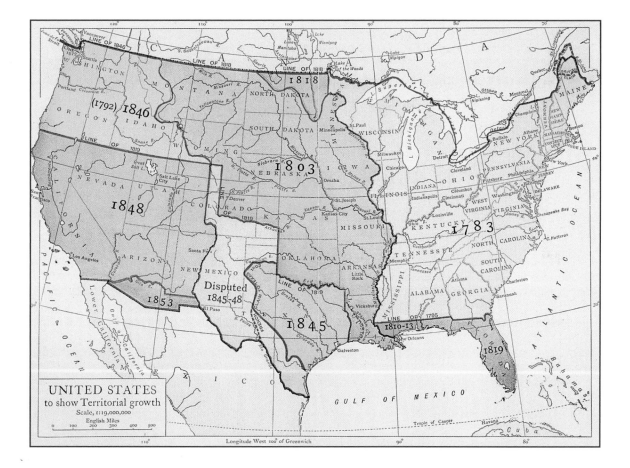

This map shows the land added to the United States during Polk's term of office — the Oregon Territory (1846), all of Texas (1845–48), and the Southwest (1848).

The new U.S. territory paid off quickly. Rumors of western gold had circulated for years. Then, in the same month the United States took official possession of California, a worker at Sutter's Mill there discovered gold nuggets in a stream. Within months, word of the gold strike reached the eastern states and set off the great California gold rush.

Gold Fever!

"The accounts of the abundance of gold in that territory are of such an extraordinary character as would scarcely command belief," President Polk said in his December 1848 message to Congress. Polk's announcement confirmed rumors of a big gold strike and sent thousands scrambling to California with dreams of striking it rich. The earliest arrivals were called "forty-niners" for the year they arrived. The nickname survives as the name of a professional football team in San Francisco, which was then California's major city.

Lawless boomtowns sprouted near rivers and streams where prospectors panned for gold. A few got rich by finding gold. Many others got nearly as rich setting up saloons, boardinghouses, and stores for the prospectors. One salesman named Levi Strauss tried to sell canvas for prospectors' tents. When that didn't work, he made the fabric into sturdy canvas trousers and found a ready market. Soon he was making the trousers of blue denim, and for generations, his family sold Levis to the nation and the world.

Within five years after the discovery of gold at Sutter's Mill, $285 million in gold had been pulled out of the California ground. California became a state in 1850, only two years after it became a U.S. territory.

☆★☆

Prospectors eager to find gold increased California's population from 10,000 to nearly 100,000 in two years. Its application for statehood in 1850 helped bring on a national crisis.

The Rise of Women's Rights

One event in the tumultuous year of 1848 did not get very much attention, but it proved to have lasting consequences for the country and its politics. In July that year, two women—Lucretia Mott and Elizabeth Cady Stanton—announced a meeting in the small town of Seneca Falls, New York, to discuss the rights of women. They were shocked when 240 people arrived, about 200 women and 40 men.

Women's roles at the time were very restricted. They could not vote or own property. Job opportunities were limited, and most girls had little opportunity for education. Their lives were almost completely controlled by men—their fathers, husbands, or brothers.

Mott and Stanton presented an imitation of the Declaration of Independence, which read, "We hold these truths to be self-evident: that all men and women are created equal." The document then listed the wrongs women suffered at the hands of men, and the rights women should have. In 1848, it was a shocking document to many men and women alike.

After that, women's national conventions were held every year. Their work was slow and there were many setbacks. It was not until 1920—72 years later—that the 19th Amendment to the Constitution gave women the right to vote in federal elections. Even today women's rights advocates trace the beginning of their movement to that meeting in 1848, when James Polk was president.

☆ ☆ ☆

The opening of western lands benefited many other groups of Americans, besides get-rich-quick gold seekers. Slave-owning cotton growers were now able to expand into Texas with the government's blessing. From west coast ports such as San Francisco, shipping and trading companies could reach China, Japan, and other Asian countries much more easily. A parade of small farmers now crossed the Mississippi and set up homesteads on free or cheap land.

The country's deep confidence in Manifest Destiny also had ugly consequences. It strained relations between the United States and Mexico for many decades and increased suspicion of the country's motives in the rest of the Americas. At home, Native Americans continued to suffer, victims of white Americans' belief in their own superiority. James Polk did not begin the removal of Native Americans from eastern states, but he was proud of the role he had in accomplishing that goal.

Missed Opportunities?

For all his ability and effort, Polk's rating as a president has suffered because of opportunities he seemed to miss. During the excitement of war and rapid expansion, the split between north and south continued to grow. Leaders from the two regions clashed more and more often over the status of slavery, states' rights, and the power of the federal government. Only a year after Polk left office, the conflict flared up over slavery in California and the rest of the Southwest. The Compromise of 1850, intended to paper over the differences once again, only made matters worse.

Could President Polk have helped to find a peaceful solution to the slavery question? Perhaps not, but he was slow to recognize the peril slavery posed to the United States. His family had always owned slaves and he grew up surrounded by the practice. He did not defend slavery as a moral issue, but he could not understand why some Americans were willing to risk the breakup of the Union and the danger of war to free enslaved blacks. His solution—that each state should decide for itself whether to allow or ban slavery—proved to be no solution at all.

Only near the end of his four-year term did he seem to glimpse the gathering danger. The split between North and South, he wrote in 1848, "must prove dangerous to the harmony if not the existence of the Union itself." His prediction proved accurate. Twelve years later, in 1860, southern states began seceding from the Union, setting the stage for the Civil War.

Many historians have come to think better of Polk in recent years. When former president Harry Truman was asked to list the best presidents of the past, he put Polk among his top choices. In his plain-speaking way, Truman summarized Polk's accomplishments. "[Polk] exercised the powers of the presidency . . . as they should be exercised," Truman said. "[He knew] exactly what he wanted to do in a specified period of time and did it, and when he got through with it he went home."

Birth:	November 2, 1795
Birthplace:	Mecklenburg County, North Carolina
Parents:	Samuel and Jane Knox Polk
Brothers & Sisters:	Jane Maria (1798–1876)
	Lydia Eliza (1800–1864)
	Franklin Ezekiel (1802–1831)
	Marshall Tate (1805–1831)
	John Lee (1807–1831)
	Naomi Tate (1809–1836)
	Ophelia Clarissa (1812–1861)
	William Hankins (1815–1862)
	Samuel Wilson (1817–1839)
Education:	University of North Carolina, graduated 1818
Occupation:	Lawyer
Marriage:	To Sarah Childress, January 1, 1824
Children:	None
Political Party:	Democratic
Public Offices:	1823–1825 Tennessee State Legislature
	1825–1839 U.S. House of Representatives
	Speaker of the House, 1835–1839
	1839–1841 Governor of Tennessee
	1845–1849 Eleventh President of the United States
His Vice President:	George M. Dallas
Major Actions as President:	1846 Acquired Oregon Territory in treaty with Great Britain
	1846 Asked Congress to declare war on Mexico over Texas
	1848 Acquired vast California and New Mexico territories from Mexico in Treaty of Guadalupe Hidalgo
Death:	June 15, 1849
Age at Death:	53 years
Burial Place:	State Capitol Grounds, Nashville, Tennessee

Fast Facts

Sarah Childress Polk

Birth:	September 4, 1803
Birthplace:	Rutherford County, Tennessee
Parents:	Colonel Joseph Childress and Elizabeth Whitsett Childress
Brothers & Sisters:	Five, two older and three younger
Education:	Studied at the Moravian Institute, Salem, North Carolina
Marriage:	To James Knox Polk, January 1, 1824
Children:	None
Firsts:	Was hostess at first Thanksgiving dinner in the White House
Died:	August 14, 1891
Age at Death:	Nearly 88 years
Burial Place:	State Capitol Grounds, Nashville, Tennessee

Timeline

1795

James Knox Polk born to Samuel and Jane Knox Polk in North Carolina, November 2.

1806

Polk family moves to Tennessee.

1812

James undergoes surgery to remove a gallstone.

1813

Attends regular school for the first time.

1816

Enrolls at the University of North Carolina.

1825

Elected to the U.S. House of Representatives; reelected six times, serving until 1839.

1833

Leads study of the Bank of the United States.

1835

Chosen as Speaker of the House.

1839

Elected governor of Tennessee.

1841

Defeated for reelection as governor.

1847

U.S. forces capture Mexico City, ending fighting in the U.S.-Mexican War.

1848

Treaty of Guadalupe Hidalgo signed February 2, ending the U.S-Mexican War; U.S. receives vast California and New Mexico territories from Mexico.

1848

Whig Zachary Taylor elected president in November.

1849

Taylor inaugurated March 5; James and Sarah Polk leave Washington.

1849

James K. Polk dies in Nashville on June 15.

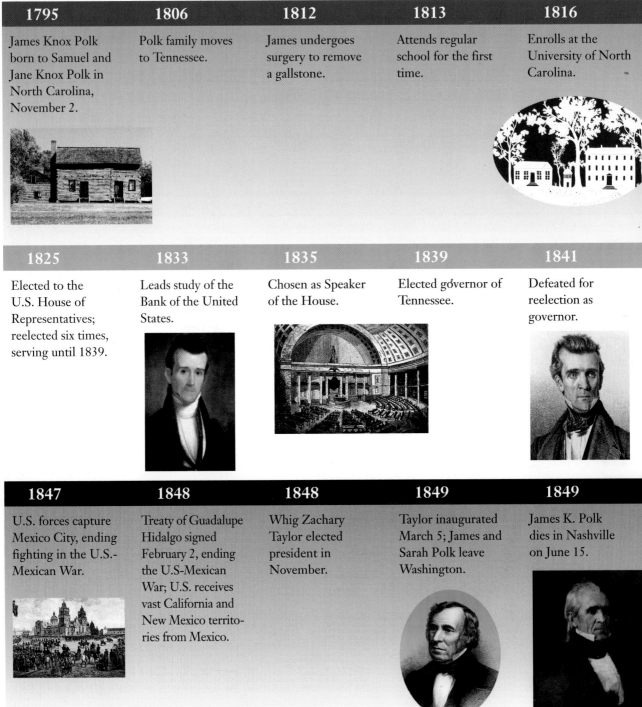

1818	1819	1820	1823	1824
Graduates from college.	Appointed clerk of the Tennessee senate.	Licensed to practice law.	Elected to Tennessee state legislature.	Marries Sarah Childress.

1843	1844	1845	1846	1846
Defeated again in campaign for governor.	Chosen as "dark-horse" Democratic candidate for president. Wins national election in November.	Inaugurated 11th U.S. president on March 4.	Signs treaty with Great Britain, giving the U.S. full control of the Oregon Territory.	Asks Congress for a declaration of war against Mexico, directs the war as commander in chief.

Glossary

abolitionist: a person who believed in the 1800s that all slavery should be ended in the United States

annex: to add territory or land

ballot: one round of voting, especially at a political convention

cabinet: directors of government departments who meet to advise the president

commander in chief: the president's role as leader of the armed forces

compromise: to give up something in order to reach an agreement

delegate: a representative at a political meeting

federal: national, not state or local

immigrants: people who have come from another country to live

import: to bring products into a country

inauguration: a ceremony to install the president

legislative: lawmaking

legislature: a body of elected representatives that makes laws for a government

majority: more than half

Manifest Destiny: a belief during the 1800s that the United States should expand across the North American continent

nomination: the naming of someone to be a candidate for an office

nullification: the theory that a state can refuse to observe national laws it considers unjust

surveyor: a person who measures land and determines boundaries

tariff: a tax, usually on goods being brought into or shipped out of a country

tax: fees charged by a government to help support its operations

unconstitutional: not permitted by the U.S. Constitution

veto: a president's refusal to sign a bill passed by Congress

Further Reading

Bramwell, Neil D. *James K. Polk*. Berkeley Heights, NJ: MyReportLinks.com Books, 2002.

Gaines, Ann Graham. *James K. Polk: Our Eleventh President*. Chanhassen, MN: Childs World, 2002.

Smalley, Ruth. *Interview with James K. Polk*. Johnson City, TN: Overmountain Press, 2002.

Tibbetts, Alison Davis. *James K. Polk*. Springfield, NJ: Enslow Publishers, 1999.

Welsbacher, Anne. *James K. Polk*. Edina, MN: Checkerboard Library, 2001.

MORE ADVANCED READING

Bumgarner, John Reed. *Sarah Childress Polk, A Biography of the Remarkable First Lady*. Jefferson, NC: McFarland & Company, 1997.

Byrnes, Mark E. *James K. Polk, A Biographical Companion*. Santa Barbara, CA: ABC-CLIO, 2001.

Haynes, Sam W. *James K. Polk and the Expansionist Impulse*. New York: Longman, 1997.

Nevin, David, et al. *The Mexican War*. Alexandria, VA: Time-Life Books, 1978.

Places to Visit

★ ★ ★ ★ ★

**James K. Polk Memorial State Historical
  Site**
Highway 521
P.O. Box 475
Pineville, NC 28134
(704) 889-7145
*http://www.ah.dcr.state.nc.us/sections/hs/
polk/polk.htm*

This memorial is near James K. Polk's birth-
place in Mecklenburg County, and features a
reconstructed log house and exhibits.

James K. Polk Home
301 West Seventh Street
P.O. Box 741
Columbia, TN 38402
(931) 388-2354
http://www.jameskpolk.com

James K. Polk lived here with his parents
from 1818 to 1824. It is now a museum with
exhibits about Polk, his family, and his
career.

The Hermitage
4580 Rachel's Lane
Nashville, TN 37076-1344
(615) 889-2941
http://www.thehermitage.com/

The Hermitage, located 12 miles east of
downtown Nashville, is the mansion of
General Andrew Jackson, the seventh U.S.
president, and James K. Polk's friend and
mentor.

**Tomb of James K. and Sarah Childress
  Polk**
Tennessee State Capitol
Charlotte Avenue
Nashville, TN

The Polks were buried on the grounds of
their home in Nashville. When the home was
torn down, they were moved to the grounds
of the Tennessee State Capitol.

The White House
1600 Pennsylvania Avenue NW
Washington, D.C. 20500
24-hour Visitors Office Info Line
(202) 456-7041

James and Sarah Polk lived here from 1845
to 1849.

Online Sites of Interest

★ **Internet Public Library, Presidents of the United States (IPL POTUS)**

http://www.ipl.org/div/potus/jkpolk.html

Includes concise information about Polk and his presidency and provides links to other sites of interest.

★ **American President.org**

http://www.americanpresident.org/history/jamespolk/

A detailed and informative biography of Polk, providing background information on his early life, family, career, and presidency. This site provides biographies of all the presidents.

★ **Grolier**

http://gi.grolier.com/presidents/

This publisher of reference material offers information on the presidents at several different reading levels, in addition to presidential portraits and information about presidential elections.

★ **The White House**

www.whitehouse.gov/history/presidents/jp11.html

Offers brief biographical articles on each president and first lady.

★ **U.S.-Mexican War**

http://www.pbs.org/kera/usmexicanwar/

Offers a wealth of information on many aspects of the war.

★ **The James K. Polk Home**

http://www.jameskpolk.com

This site provides views of the home of Polk and his family in Columbia, Tennessee, and offers additional information about his life and presidency.

For other interesting sites, see those listed in *Places to Visit* on page 102.

Table of Presidents

1. George Washington **2. John Adams** **3. Thomas Jefferson** **4. James Madison**

	1. George Washington	2. John Adams	3. Thomas Jefferson	4. James Madison
Took office	Apr 30 1789	Mar 4 1797	Mar 4 1801	Mar 4 1809
Left office	Mar 3 1797	Mar 3 1801	Mar 3 1809	Mar 3 1817
Birthplace	Westmoreland Co, VA	Braintree, MA	Shadwell, VA	Port Conway, VA
Birth date	Feb 22 1732	Oct 20 1735	Apr 13 1743	Mar 16 1751
Death date	Dec 14 1799	July 4 1826	July 4 1826	June 28 1836

9. William H. Harrison **10. John Tyler** **11. James K. Polk** **12. Zachary Taylor**

	9. William H. Harrison	10. John Tyler	11. James K. Polk	12. Zachary Taylor
Took office	Mar 4 1841	Apr 6 1841	Mar 4 1845	Mar 5 1849
Left office	Apr 4 1841•	Mar 3 1845	Mar 3 1849	July 9 1850•
Birthplace	Berkeley, VA	Greenway, VA	Mecklenburg Co, NC	Barboursville, VA
Birth date	Feb 9 1773	Mar 29 1790	Nov 2 1795	Nov 24 1784
Death date	Apr 4 1841	Jan 18 1862	June 15 1849	July 9 1850

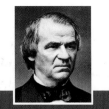    

17. Andrew Johnson **18. Ulysses S. Grant** **19. Rutherford B. Hayes** **20. James A. Garfield**

	17. Andrew Johnson	18. Ulysses S. Grant	19. Rutherford B. Hayes	20. James A. Garfield
Took office	Apr 15 1865	Mar 4 1869	Mar 4 1877	Mar 4 1881
Left office	Mar 3 1869	Mar 3 1877	Mar 3 1881	Sept 19 1881•
Birthplace	Raleigh, NC	Point Pleasant, OH	Delaware, OH	Orange, OH
Birth date	Dec 29 1808	Apr 27 1822	Oct 4 1822	Nov 19 1831
Death date	July 31 1875	July 23 1885	Jan 17 1893	Sept 19 1881

5. James Monroe	6. John Quincy Adams	7. Andrew Jackson	8. Martin Van Buren
Mar 4 1817	Mar 4 1825	Mar 4 1829	Mar 4 1837
Mar 3 1825	Mar 3 1829	Mar 3 1837	Mar 3 1841
Westmoreland Co, VA	Braintree, MA	The Waxhaws, SC	Kinderhook, NY
Apr 28 1758	July 11 1767	Mar 15 1767	Dec 5 1782
July 4 1831	Feb 23 1848	June 8 1845	July 24 1862

13. Millard Fillmore	14. Franklin Pierce	15. James Buchanan	16. Abraham Lincoln
July 9 1850	Mar 4 1853	Mar 4 1857	Mar 4 1861
Mar 3 1853	Mar 3 1857	Mar 3 1861	Apr 15 1865•
Locke Township, NY	Hillsborough, NH	Cove Gap, PA	Hardin Co, KY
Jan 7 1800	Nov 23 1804	Apr 23 1791	Feb 12 1809
Mar 8 1874	Oct 8 1869	June 1 1868	Apr 15 1865

21. Chester A. Arthur	22. Grover Cleveland	23. Benjamin Harrison	24. Grover Cleveland
Sept 19 1881	Mar 4 1885	Mar 4 1889	Mar 4 1893
Mar 3 1885	Mar 3 1889	Mar 3 1893	Mar 3 1897
Fairfield, VT	Caldwell, NJ	North Bend, OH	Caldwell, NJ
Oct 5 1830	Mar 18 1837	Aug 20 1833	Mar 18 1837
Nov 18 1886	June 24 1908	Mar 13 1901	June 24 1908

	25. William McKinley	26. Theodore Roosevelt	27. William H. Taft	28. Woodrow Wilson
Took office	Mar 4 1897	Sept 14 1901	Mar 4 1909	Mar 4 1913
Left office	**Sept 14 1901•**	Mar 3 1909	Mar 3 1913	Mar 3 1921
Birthplace	Niles, OH	New York, NY	Cincinnati, OH	Staunton, VA
Birth date	Jan 29 1843	Oct 27 1858	Sept 15 1857	Dec 28 1856
Death date	Sept 14 1901	Jan 6 1919	Mar 8 1930	Feb 3 1924

	33. Harry S. Truman	34. Dwight D. Eisenhower	35. John F. Kennedy	36. Lyndon B. Johnson
Took office	Apr 12 1945	Jan 20 1953	Jan 20 1961	Nov 22 1963
Left office	Jan 20 1953	Jan 20 1961	**Nov 22 1963•**	Jan 20 1969
Birthplace	Lamar, MO	Denison, TX	Brookline, MA	Johnson City, TX
Birth date	May 8 1884	Oct 14 1890	May 29 1917	Aug 27 1908
Death date	Dec 26 1972	Mar 28 1969	Nov 22 1963	Jan 22 1973

	41. George Bush	42. Bill Clinton	43. George W. Bush
Took office	Jan 20 1989	Jan 20 1993	Jan 20 2001
Left office	Jan 20 1993	Jan 20 2001	—
Birthplace	Milton, MA	Hope, AR	New Haven, CT
Birth date	June 12 1924	Aug 19 1946	July 6 1946
Death date	—	—	—

29. Warren G. Harding	30. Calvin Coolidge	31. Herbert Hoover	32. Franklin D. Roosevelt
Mar 4 1921	Aug 2 1923	Mar 4 1929	Mar 4 1933
Aug 2 1923•	Mar 3 1929	Mar 3 1933	**Apr 12 1945•**
Blooming Grove, OH	Plymouth, VT	West Branch, IA	Hyde Park, NY
Nov 21 1865	July 4 1872	Aug 10 1874	Jan 30 1882
Aug 2 1923	Jan 5 1933	Oct 20 1964	Apr 12 1945

37. Richard M. Nixon	38. Gerald R. Ford	39. Jimmy Carter	40. Ronald Reagan
Jan 20 1969	Aug 9 1974	Jan 20 1977	Jan 20 1981
Aug 9 1974★	Jan 20 1977	Jan 20 1981	Jan 20 1989
Yorba Linda, CA	Omaha, NE	Plains, GA	Tampico, IL
Jan 9 1913	July 14 1913	Oct 1 1924	Feb 11 1911
Apr 22 1994	—	—	—

• Indicates the president died while in office.
★ Richard Nixon resigned before his term expired.

Index

★ ★ ★ ★ ★

Page numbers in *italics* indicate illustrations.

About the Author

The author, Sean McCollum, believes James K. Polk has not received the attention the eleventh U.S. president merits, and thinks the Polk presidency has valuable lessons to teach Americans today. Sean found President Polk's presidential diary a terrific resource, full of insights into a very ambitious, determined, and disciplined politician and leader.

Sean loves writing for kids, and learning along with them. He has published eleven books and hundreds of magazine articles. He is a regular contributor to *Boys' Life*, *Junior Scholastic*, the *New York Times Upfront*, and *National Geographic Kids*. He has traveled to more than 40 countries, but lives in the mountains near Boulder, Colorado, where he's visited daily by foxes, woodpeckers, and a mule deer named Bucket.